"It's Not a Bug, It's a Feature!"

Computer Wit and Wisdom

Compiled by David Lubar

ADDISON-WESLEY PUBLISHING COMPANY

Reading, Massachusetts • Menlo Park, California • New York
Don Mills, Ontario • Wokingham, England • Amsterdam
Bonn • Sydney • Singapore • Tokyo • Madrid • San Juan
Paris • Seoul • Milan • Mexico City • Taipei

Many of the designations used by manufacturers and sellers to distinguish their products are claimed as trademarks. Where those designations appear in this book, and Addison-Wesley was aware of a trademark claim, the designations have been printed in initial capital letters or all capital letters.

The authors and publishers have taken care in preparation of this book, but make no expressed or implied warranty of any kind and assume no responsibility for errors or omissions. No liability is assumed for incidental or consequential damages in connection with or arising out of the use of the information or programs contained herein.

Library of Congress Cataloging-in-Publication Data

Lubar, David.

It's not a bug, it's a feature : computer wit and wisdom / compiled by David Lubar.

p.   cm.

ISBN 0-201-48304-1

1. Computers—Miscellanea.   I. Title.

QA76.5.L75   1995   94-44614

004—dc20   CIP

Sponsoring Editor: Kathleen Tibbetts
Project Manager: Sarah Weaver
Cover design: Jean Seal
Text design: Greg Johnson, *Art Directions*
Set in 12 point Goudy by Greg Johnson, *Art Directions*

1 2 3 4 5 6 7 8 9 -DOH- 99 98 97 96 95
First printing, February 1995

Addison-Wesley books are available for bulk purchases by corporations, institutions, and other organizations. For more information please contact the Corporate, Government, and Special Sales Department at (800) 238-9682.

*For Joelle, who understood
about that first computer.*

Acknowledgments

With the notable exception of *Autobiography of a Dust Mite*, few books have been written in a vacuum. I received much help, in many ways, during the creation of this modest volume. I'd like to take space here to thank the people who lent a hand. It's cheaper than gifts. Thanks to Claudette Moore for patience, wisdom, and a sense of humor. Thanks to Kathleen Tibbetts, an editor who was delightful to work with, for providing a gentle prod whenever I wandered off the path. Thanks to Joelle for doing all the real work around the house while I got to sit and write. Thanks to Alison for offering to help, and for reminding me that no book is the center of the universe. For many reasons, thanks to all the following: TOM WONG (who was so helpful I promised him capital letters), Jim Vanecek, Fred Fedorko, Jack Namba, Jon Lubar, Dave and Judie Pearson, Frank Covitz, Doug Baldwin, Tom and Donna Roginski, John and Elaine Snyder, Marilyn Gomes, and MaryAnn Tasillo. Special thanks to David Ahl for giving me my first job in the industry many years ago. Thanks to Ted Nelson for making it interesting, bizarre, and occasionally frightening. Thanks to the Greater Lehigh Valley Writers Group for enthusiasm and support. Thanks to every librarian in the world, and especially those in reference departments. All the thanks in the world to my mother, Lisbet Lubar, who taught me to love research. Thanks to Benjamin Goldenberg for influencing me in more ways than he ever knew. Thanks to all the dreamers who made the dream affordable. Finally, thanks to all the brilliant people whose words appear here. Thanks for the wit and the insight.

David Lubar

Contents

Computers
Are Easy

Using a computer is just like riding a bike, except you don't have to wear the tight shorts and funny helmet. A water bottle is also inadvisable. Just about everyone agrees that computing is incredibly simple, or will be in only a few more days. Listen to what the experts have to say . . . .

A ny nitwit can understand computers, and many do.

Ted Nelson, visionary
and radical computerist, 1974

V ery candidly, I don't expect this new tutorial to teach me how to set a clock on the VCR or anything complicated.

George Bush, announcing his plans
to become computer literate, 1991

T he future masters of technology will have to be lighthearted and intelligent. The machine easily masters the grim and the dumb.

Marshall McLuhan, 1969

A brand new computer! Oh joy! New things to learn. New, bewildering instructions to follow. Ordinarily, I'd rather be shot.

Daniel Pinkwater, upon being asked to evaluate a new "plug and play" PC, 1994

In the land of relativity, WordPerfect is easy to use compared to WordStar, which is really a snap compared to XyWrite, which is a breeze compared to intestinal surgery.

Christopher O'Malley, 1992

3

Life is too short to hassle with the results of other people's laziness. You pay good money for a program, and you shouldn't end up lost and wondering what to do. If a program makes you feel stupid, it's not because you are; it's because the person who wrote the program is.

Arthur Naiman, 1985

This model is even easier to use since it doesn't come loaded down with a whole bunch of software.

Salesperson in a computer store, 1994

But for all its vaunted ease of use, there's not much about a Mac that's intuitive either. Unless you've watched someone click and drag, the mouse might as well be a bar of soap.

Joel Dreyfuss, 1994

The profusion of sophisticated hardware and software that *works* today is absolutely amazing! We still can't understand the instructions, but that is another story.

David Lien, 1984

If you are having trouble running your favorite computer program, all of the experts seem to agree that there is a good chance it is your own fault.

Alan Serchuk, 1990

Nobody Needs One

Ever since a group of ancient Phoenicians argued that the use of the sail would cause the rowing public to grow fat and lazy, man has had a tradition of resisting technology. But you may as well try to stop a steamroller with a spitball. Technology tries to crush what it cannot move. Eventually, even if you have absolutely no need for a computer, you will own one. And you will wonder how you ever lived without it. Several days later, something better will come along.

For most of human history counting was scarcely necessary; computing was irrelevant. It did not matter much if there was one wolf outside or if there were seven; one saber-toothed tiger was as necessary to avoid as four.

Joel Shurkin, 1984

In truth, no one really needs a computer until the day he gets one.

Jean-Louis Gassée, 1987

Machines, technology, computers—hah! They're all overrated. When you want something done right, let a person do it.

Duckman, 1994

Machines will always be better than people. People get angry, they make mistakes, they fail, but computers never fail. They're perfect.

Mambo and Charles, Duckman's two-headed son, 1994

With the possible exception of a careless machinist who has lost all but one finger to accidents, humans have little need or use for a number system based solely on 1 and 0.

Peter Stoler on the binary system, 1984

Data is flying around, across, and through your systems at speeds the Jetsons could appreciate, but has any of this technology let you go home one minute early? I doubt it.

Richard Santalesa, 1992

It's reassuring that even in this computer age talented, individual people often do better than the whole vast machinery of national weather services in predicting critical changes in weather.

Gerard K. O'Neill, 1981

Large numbers of people hung up their computing shoes after just a few months of experimentation with their new toys. They discovered to their genuine dismay that word processors do not write letters by themselves, spreadsheets do not make entries in checkbooks, and that maintaining data bases of recipes isn't such a hot idea after all.

Arlan R. Levitan, 1984

How many times can you see your overdrawn checkbook converted into a sine wave before the thrill wears off?

Gregg Easterbrook, 1983

. . . the typical home doesn't have much information that needs to be processed.

John Case, 1985

Any fool can think of wonderful ways to use a computer, but it takes intelligence to think of the consequences, the overall costs, and the possibilities for eventual trouble.

Fred Joseph Gruenberger, 1975

Who has such a large Christmas card mailing list that you need to keep it on a computer? If so, why aren't I on it?

David D. Thornburg, 1985

The Early Years

Once, parents hounded their children with tales of walking miles to school in six feet of snow. That was before global warming took away all the snow. Fortunately, we have the computer to help fill the gap in hardship stories. The real old-timers can spend entire evenings spinning nostalgic recollections of vacuum tubes and punch cards. The rest of us will have to make do reminiscing about the traumas we experienced before CD-ROMs came preinstalled.

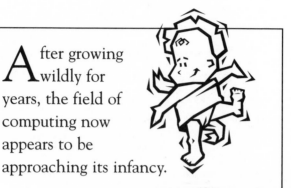

After growing wildly for years, the field of computing now appears to be approaching its infancy.

The President's Science Advisory Committee, 1967

In the old days, you had to hassle with front panels, hardwiring and hand entering monitor programs and cassette I/O routines via switches and numeric key pads. Nowadays, the hardest part is opening the bubble package the software comes in.

Michael Shrayer, author of one of the first word processors for personal computers, 1984

15

The Univac test technicians, and later we students, discovered that the cooling coils under the false floor of the computer made excellent refrigerators for soft drinks or beer.

David E. Lundstrom, 1988

Most people first became personally aware of computers in the early 1960s, when strange-looking numerals began appearing on their checks, or they began getting bills on punched cards and were sternly warned not to fold, spindle or mutilate the cards. Something unspecified but probably horrible was supposed to happen if you crumpled your electric bill.

Daniel Cohen, 1975

The radical element of the first computer built was not its speed but the effort to have 18,000 parts functioning almost simultaneously.

Ralph I. Cole, 1969

Whirlwind I, a pioneering computer of the 1950s, cost $5 million. Machines with the same computing power can now be purchased for $20.

James Martin, 1978

Never trust a computer you can't pick up.

Anonymous homage to small computers

At the time of this writing, APF offers no peripherals for the IM–1. But, by April, the company hopes to offer floppy-disk, printer, memory expansion and communications modem additions.

David B. Powell, in a review of the rather limited Imagination Machine from APF Electronics, 1980

There was a time when the fastest way to move a lot of information from one place to another sixty miles away was load a station wagon with magnetic tape and drive for an hour.

Bennett Falk, 1994

18

If the Apple beeps and garbage appears but you cannot see an "*" and the cursor, the horizontal or vertical settings on the TV need to be adjusted. Now depress and release the "ESC" key, then hold down the "SHIFT" key while depressing and releasing the P key. This should clear your TV screen to all black. Now depress and release the "RESET" key again. The "*" prompt character and the cursor should return to the lower left of your TV screen.

The Apple II Reference Manual (the Red Book), giving instructions for turning on the computer, 1978

Software

You can never have enough software. By the time you've accumulated all you want or need, there'll be updates for most of it. Some updates are free, except for a small shipping and handling fee of $49.95. Does anyone know where you go to apply for a job as a handler? The great thing about software is that it allows a computer to do almost anything. Actually, this isn't quite true. In reality, software allows a computer to do anything—almost. It can almost handle your finances, except for special situations like that limited partnership in first-edition Garfield prints that Uncle Phil swore would double in value. It can almost print your newsletter, but only after it swallows your best paragraph. It can almost run a business, but not without sending bills for $00.00 or mailing ads to Mr. Rutgers University.

The software and data on this CD has no guarantee of any type whatsoever.

Disclaimer on a CD-ROM, 1992

And all of my free programs come with a money-back guarantee.

Jim Butterfield, early Commodore software superstar, 1983

This software is licensed "as is." The entire risk as to the quality and performance of the software is with the buyer.

Disclaimer from a utility program, 1985

An omelette, promised in two minutes, may appear to be progressing nicely. But when it has not set in two minutes, the customer has two choices—wait or eat it raw. Software customers have had the same choice.

Frederick P. Brooks, Jr., 1975

. . . don't assume that just because a utility or add-in program is available, it's worthwhile. Utilities are meant to be problem solvers. If there's no problem, chances are pretty good you don't need a solution.

Barry Owen, 1991

... we forget that you cannot impress software, no matter what your rank.

Rear Admiral Grace Hopper, who helped design COBOL and coined the word "bug," circa 1970

Software is what makes your computer behave and look smarter than it is.

Winn Schwartau, 1994

... most programs are more like Verdi operas; they communicate in a foreign language and require reading notes in advance to have any idea of what is happening.

Paul Heckel, 1982

23

To make a mint on software, just think. Think alone, if you can, or at worst with a tiny team of fellow nerds. Write a program that helps other people think better—a spreadsheet, a database, an electronic checkbook. Run off a million copies on floppy disks, at a cost of a buck or two each. Then sell them for $195 plus tax.

Peter Huber, 1993

Suites are the software industry's version of multiple-course meals. They won't block your arteries; however, they will clog your hard disk.

Lawrence Magid, 1994

Leonardo da Vinci called music "the shaping of the invisible," and his phrase is even more apt as a description of software.

Alan Kay, who helped create the mouse, the concept of windows, and a few other things, 1984

Programmers often neglect proper consideration of the weak link in the software: the person who will be using it.

Leonard Lee, 1992

Serving Our New Master: The Computer Conquers the World

After the baby boomers recovered from the trauma of air raid drills and the fear of giant mutant ants rising from the radioactive ruins of a nuclear experiment gone wrong, they discovered a new terror. The latest attempt of science to end mankind's rule of the planet came in a box—it hummed, it whirred, it flashed, and it knew what was best for everyone.

We fear what we do not understand, and so ordinary people fear computers more than they fear filing cabinets . . .

F. J. M. Laver, 1980

. . . there is reason to hope that the machines will use us kindly, for their existence will be in a great measure dependent on ours; they will rule us with a rod of iron, but they will not eat us . . .

Samuel Butler, 1872

Hal was what we were afraid the IBM 360 would become in the 1980's.

Jerry Willis, discussing the computer from 2001: A Space Odyssey, 1978

If computers ever control people it will not be because human minds are less intelligent than machines but because they are lazier.

Walter Buckingham, 1961

Maybe it ought to sound like Jackie Mason.

Stanley Kubrick, speculating on the voice of HAL, circa 1968

And to this end they built themselves a stupendous super computer which was so amazingly intelligent that even before its data banks had been connected up it had started from *I think therefore I am* and got as far as deducing the existence of rice pudding and income tax before anyone managed to turn it off.

Douglas Adams, describing Deep Thought in The Hitchhiker's Guide to the Galaxy, *1979*

If we distrust the computer, it is because we distrust ourselves and what we do with our machines.

Eugene F. Provenzo, 1986

It's not very likely that we'll suddenly be presented with a giant conglomeration of hardware and software and told, "Here is your new leader."

George Johnson, 1986

. . . one can always pull out the computer's power plug. But the nagging idea that a computer might someday develop a will of its own, and put its power plug back is the modern version of an ancient superstition.

Donald G. Fink, 1966

It would be nice to see a sci-fi movie that catches up with the current engineering realities and allows a pea-sized brain to rule the Earth. (I know, some think that that's already happened.)

Srully Blotnick, 1984

You Stupid Piece of Junk!

People have been dealing with stupid machines for centuries. It is especially delightful to learn that even "thinking" machines are quite stupid. The computer has more in common with the toaster than with the terrier. We can remain smug for the moment.

Computers are so obedient that, even if the instructions you give them are completely nonsensical, the computer will carry them out to the letter.

John G. Kemeny, 1972

When asked to set fire to the logs in your fireplace, a friend will oblige cheerfully. Asked to set fire to your house, the friend will at least say, "Are you quite sure?" Is this kind of behavior too much to ask of a computer?

John Shore, 1985

We know that the most advanced computer in the world does not have a brain as sophisticated as that of an ant. True, we could say that of many of our relatives but we only have to put up with them at weddings or special occasions.

Woody Allen, circa 1977

Often what we tell a computer is different from what we think we are telling it.

Fred D'Ignazio, 1984

Always remember that computers are machines. They are tools, mechanical devices. And just as you can drive an automobile without knowing how to build one, you can use your computer without knowing how to assemble it. Your computer is a moron or less. We assume that you are not that limited.

Frank Herbert, 1980

Deep down in their innermost workings, computers are incredibly simpleminded. (Their redeeming feature is that they are very, very fast. Any simpleton who can do millions of calculations per minute is not to be sneezed at.)

Joseph Deken, 1981

35

They are not very smart by biological standards in spite of their impressive specialized abilities. Perhaps their IQ is about on par with the IQ of a Cambrian mudworm.

O. B. Hardison Jr., 1989

The computer will do the same thing the same way every time—right or wrong! That is why it is possible to pay every employee wrong on the same payday, produce hundreds of bad invoices in a matter of minutes, or destroy an entire file as quickly as it can be read.

William E. Perry, 1989

Computers have proved adept at handling abstract challenges like flying spaceships, playing chess, and solving quadratic equations, but housework is too hard.

Timothy Ferris, 1993

Cast of Characters, Part One: Entrepreneurs, Inventors, and Pioneers

Charles Babbage attempted to build a computer more than 150 years ago. Had he waited until *Computer Shopper* was published, the task would have been significantly easier. Over the last few decades, an array of brilliant people improved the computer, making it faster and smaller. Eventually, it will become so small that it will no longer require a dust cover. The people who make dust covers will switch to making little beepers that will help the user locate the computer. As always, someone will step in to fill a need, even before it exists.

When a man splits a grain of sand and the universe is turned upside down in consequence, it is difficult to realize that to the man who did it, the splitting of the grain is the great affair, and the capsizing of the cosmos quite a small one.

G. K. Chesterton, 1905

I submit to the public a small machine by my invention, by means of which you alone may, without any effort, perform all the operations of arithmetic, and may be relieved of the work which has often times fatigued your spirit . . .

Blaise Pascal (1623–1662)

Like many visionaries, Babbage underestimated the power of his own vision.

Jeremy Bernstein, 1982

If IBM is God in the PC universe then Bill Gates is the pope.

Robert X. Cringely, 1992

I couldn't even afford a garage.

Sandra L. Kurtzig, describing the early entrepreneurial days of ASK Computer Systems, 1991

D o you want to go on selling sugar water, or do you want a chance to change the world?

Attributed in various forms to Steve Jobs when he asked John Sculley to leave Pepsi for Apple, 1983

Y ou have to be prepared to fail, and I have failed about half the time, I guess. But you simply have to pick yourself up and go at it again with whatever insights you've gained from failure. If you do keep trying, you will occasionally do something worthwhile.

Seymour Cray, supercomputer designer, 1994

We are the salvation of the world. If you market the tools for salvation, you have to be incompetent not to make money.

> Andy Grove, co-founder of
> Intel Corporation, circa 1984

The minute you're through changing, you're through.

> Jack Tramiel, founder of
> Commodore International, 1983

This machine cost me a full week's work to bring it to perfection.

> Robinson Crusoe, as reported by Daniel Defoe
> in an early exercise in R&D costs, 1719

The goal was that it had to be better than the back of an envelope.

Dan Bricklin, creator of VisiCalc, circa 1978

Not one American in ten thousand could name the two countrymen who invented the integrated circuit and launched the Second Industrial Revolution.

T. R. Reid, discussing Jack Kilby and Bob Noyce, 1984

It wasn't a sensation.

Jack Kilby, co-inventor of the integrated circuit, describing the first public reaction to the device in 1959

The first time is black magic, then it becomes routine.

Chuck Moore, chip designer and creator of the FORTH language, on emerging technologies, 1992

Operating Systems, Languages, and Other Sacraments

There are only two types of operating systems in the world: yours and the inferior ones. Any programmer will tell you there are also only two kinds of programming languages: his and the inefficient ones. Of course, since an operating system is just a program, things can get a bit sticky. And since a programming language runs under an operating system. . . Never mind.

The assorted loony bigots who so bedevil the world are far more dangerous, and absolutely unforgivable, but they don't have anything on the True Computer Believer when it comes to intolerance.

Sam Waterman, 1993

From time to time, contractors are accosted by what seem to be religious zealots. They are really just Apple Macintosh users.

Bill Smith

Many people do not merely respect IBM. They *believe* in IBM. This leads one to suspect that perhaps IBM should not be seen as a company at all. It is much more like a religion.

Ted Nelson, 1977

. . . there are Mac zealots to whom IBM is a four-letter word.

Mark Alvarez, 1990

I felt like an entrepreneur flaunting Levis in Red Square.

Michael Maren, bringing his Macintosh
to a PC office, 1990

Even Microsoft couldn't build a successful marketing campaign around the slogan: "Unlike the 50 million copies we've already sold you, this version actually works!"

Paul Bonner, reviewing Windows 4.0, or Chicago, or Windows 95, or whatever it's called this week, 1994

DOS is like the faithful worker who's agreed to delay retirement. He'd love it if the company would bring in some younger blood, but they can't seem to find anyone to replace him.

Scott Spanbauer, 1992

Fortran fans like to say Fortran will never die—because whatever they're using 10 years from now, they'll call it Fortran.

Michael E. McCarthy, 1994

Machine language is easy to read—if you're a machine.

Ken Skier, 1981

Because every person knows what he likes, every person thinks he is an expert on user interfaces.

Paul Heckel, 1982

I have a theory—as yet unproven—that the average executive might start to resent being treated like a child by the unspoken assumption, inherent in icons, that he can understand pictures but not words.

Peter Rodwell, 1984

Why would anyone in their right mind use Windows for anything? You can always buy a slower computer if yours is too fast!

John McCormick, 1990

No matter how hard you try, a desktop interface will never be a desk.

Gene Callahan, 1994

If God had meant for man to use Windows, he would have given him more patience.

Jacques Hughes, 1993

Every DOS program that has sold more than 100 copies has been ported to Windows or is well into the planning stage for the big move (that is, the T-shirt is already done).

Sam Waterman, 1992

"This will end your Windows session." I live for those six words.

Anonymous

Bugs and Glitches

If it weren't for bugs, the average computer program could be written in about two hours and thirty minutes. Add a few bugs and the process expands to eight or nine months. Generally, a glitch is a bug in hardware, while a bug is a glitch in software. On the last day of the quarter, when your data vanishes forever, it doesn't matter which term you use. In the early years, users expected lots of bugs. Somewhere along the line, this tolerance evaporated. A bug can be subtle; it might just throw your checking balance off by a penny a month. A bug can be brutal; it might cut off all long-distance service for half the country. The worst bugs pop-up only rarely, making them hard to detect and fix. Fortunately, most programming teams are large enough so there is always someone else to blame.

Computers can be lousy with bugs, so thick with them that one suspects—in the ultimate nightmare—that bugs are shuttling back and forth at will from software to hardware.

Thomas A. Bass

It's supposed to do that.

Anonymous help-line response, 1982

Every really large and significant program has "just one more bug."

Gerald M. Weinberg, 1971

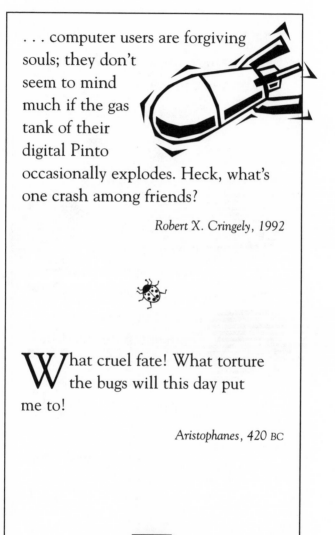

. . . computer users are forgiving souls; they don't seem to mind much if the gas tank of their digital Pinto occasionally explodes. Heck, what's one crash among friends?

Robert X. Cringely, 1992

What cruel fate! What torture the bugs will this day put me to!

Aristophanes, 420 BC

While computers are not likely to make mistakes, people are. And people control the computers.

Fred Joseph Gruenberger, 1975

When a clerk at the local power company or at your favorite department store or in your company's payroll department says, "The computer made a mistake," you have reason to assume that either that person is stupid or thinks you are.

Marvin Grosswirth, 1978

I t's not a bug, it's a feature.

> *Many sources, often heard when*
> *a product is late or already released*
> *before the bug is discovered*

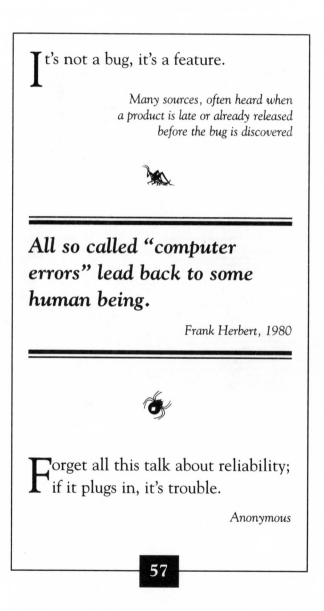

All so called "computer errors" lead back to some human being.

> *Frank Herbert, 1980*

F orget all this talk about reliability; if it plugs in, it's trouble.

> *Anonymous*

W hen you have eliminated the impossible, whatever remains, however improbable, must be the truth.

Sherlock Holmes, who would have been a world-class debugger had he come along later and been a real person, 1890

The Home
Office

The computer has brought about a revolution in work habits. Now, instead of hovering around a company-owned water cooler, the telecommuting worker can hover around his own refrigerator. Instead of a photo of the family, the kids themselves can sit on your desk. All day. The money saved on gas and tolls can help pay for part of the phone bill. Our whole way of working has changed. We will never go outdoors again.

As long as the general population attributes magical qualities to the computer, and as long as most people assume computers are far beyond their own ability to understand and operate, more business opportunities will exist for those who know the truth.

Stuart Feldstein on opportunities for the home-based entrepreneur, 1981

. . . it is a safe bet that some people will find they married their spouses not only for better or worse, but also for lunch.

T. A. Heppenheimer, discussing the future of telecommuting, 1983

*When you're at home
with technology, you're home
alone.*

*Headline in a direct mail ad
for* Computer Life, *1994*

Fellow workers may not really
believe telecommuters actually
work when they're at home.
And until they lay the law down,
they become the neighborhood
dropoff for UPS or the emergency
babysitter.

Brad Schepp, 1990

In the future, computer technology will transform the office from a piece of real estate into a mindscape . . .

Robert Kavner, 1990

Before operating this unit, please read these instructions completely.

Front cover of a printer manual, 1991

Any details given in these Operating Instructions are subject to change without notice.

Inside front cover of the same manual

... the occupational hazard of the self-employed, home-based symbolic analyst of the 1990s is isolation. Information age hunters and gatherers were lone wolves until we found the Net.

Howard Rheingold, 1993

If you are perceived to be working hard (even if you are shuffling papers ineffectually at a desk), you are likely to win more brownie points than the unseen person who excels in producing excellent work in less time and with less effort.

Patricia B. Seybold on the perils of telecommuting, 1994

It's a jungle out there, and running a business without the right tools—computers, printers, fax machines, and more—is like wandering into a lion's den wearing a lamb chop necktie.

Daniel Tynan, 1993

Wall Street

The greatest computer game on the planet evolved when Wall Street met the mainframe. The home version is just as much fun. A computer can help select stocks, thus replacing clumsy mechanical devices such as the dartboard. A computer company can go public. Several dozen seem to do so every day. A few even have earnings. It doesn't matter; your computer will tell you which ones to buy.

Investing without computerized assistance will in time resemble travel by foot as against car, train or plane.

Gerald M. Loeb, 1971

Whether, indeed, the computer will ever be able to tame to any significant degree the capricious behavior of the market is in many minds a decidedly moot question. The point, however, is that more and more traders are latching on to the computer, *believing* that it will. And this in itself is a force to be reckoned with.

Dana L. Thomas, 1967

The phenomenal success of IBM and a few other companies was bound to produce a spate of public offerings of new issues in their fields, for which large losses were virtually guaranteed.

Benjamin Graham, the father of fundamental analysis, 1973

The beauty of screening stocks with computers is that additional criteria can be added to the program indefinitely, until the only stocks the computer has left are those that match the individual investor's needs and wishes perfectly.

Brendan Boyd, 1982

Putting your financial future in the hands of a PC may seem a bit like letting your wackiest aunt have a crack at deciphering a WIN.INI file.

Gregg Keizer, 1994

Connecting to Reality.

Reality's Smart Investor gives this message when logging on, 1993

Now even computers are slowing down, at least in the mainframe and minicomputer part of the business. IBM and Digital may be the slow growers of tomorrow.

Peter Lynch, a successful investor, 1989

If you use all this financial information diligently, you may even make money. Especially if the market goes up.

William J. Cook, describing various stock trading and data software, 1984

The computer is a godsend in holding and manipulating huge amounts of data, but the day the computer will relieve the analyst of the need for shoe leather, plant inspections, character assessment, industry knowledge, and a lifetime's experience and flair will be the day birds become willing to fly up the barrel of your gun.

John Train, 1983

Parts and Peripherals

Computers are creatures of many parts. Some parts are simple. Life forms as low as the earthworm can be taught to tell a RAM chip from a hunk of beef jerky. Other parts are so complex that even their creators have no idea what they have made. By general agreement, we pay more for these.

But for all their complexity, chips also resemble the state of California in being made essentially of sand.

George Gilder, 1989

The opposed thumb is one of the defining characteristics of our species, and mine are strongly opposed to working pointing devices.

Bill Machrone, commenting on track balls, 1993

Twisted pair ain't no rock group.

Steve Gilliland, describing a standard type of communications wiring, 1994

A computer with a modem is just a computer with a modem if the computer doesn't have another computer to talk to.

Elizabeth M. Ferrarini, 1985

Humans do not naturally communicate by moving a device around on a tabletop.

Ronald D. Rotstein, speaking of mice, 1990

I know that every computer has exactly the same available memory: too little.

Ken Skier, 1981

Like everyone else, I hate modems. They are infuriating, complicated, obscure, etc., etc. But mostly they are slow. No matter how fast they are, they are slow. And slowness is the ultimate crime in computing.

Stewart Alsop, 1994

A hundred years from now, tapes will probably still be used in the movies, even if they're no longer used in reality. How else will the people in the theater know that the Giant Brain is "thinking" if they don't see blinking lights and spinning tapes?

Srully Blotnick, 1984

It's a poor sort of memory that only works backwards.

The White Queen, critiquing the human form of RAM, 1872

To my knowledge, IBM entered the market as the *only* personal computer manufacturer to promote a keyboard design that had been tried and rejected by the customers of several other computer manufacturers.

David D. Thornburg, describing the "Chicklet™" keyboard on the PCjr, 1984

The Business World

The computer has freed the worker to do his job. Mostly, it has accomplished this by keeping the bulk of managers at their desks staring at spreadsheet projections, allowing the rest of us to get something done for a change. The first business to use computers was the computer business. Its projections told it that no one would buy a computer.

A paperless office is as likely as a paperless bathroom.

Anonymous

Technology is dominated by two types of people: those who understand what they do not manage and those who manage what they do not understand.

Archibald Putt, 1981

Nobody was ever fired for buying IBM.

Anonymous

One of the promises of the early computer era was that many dull and repetitive tasks would be taken over by the machine, and indeed they have. But many of the new computer-related tasks are very nearly as dull and repetitive as the tasks they replaced.

Daniel Cohen, 1975

As one industrialist wryly observed, the really smart way to make use of a computer was to order it for delivery in eighteen months, reorganize the entire business to get ready for it, and then cancel the order.

Jean Ford Brennan, 1967

In many companies, "PC Power User" has become one of the tags hung on people who know so much about PCs that they no longer have time to learn much about their jobs.

Jim Seymour, 1991

Twenty-five-plus years of data processing experience has taught us how to do data processing right. However, one need only observe the frequency and intensity of automobile accidents to understand that knowing how to do it right and doing it right are two entirely different aspects.

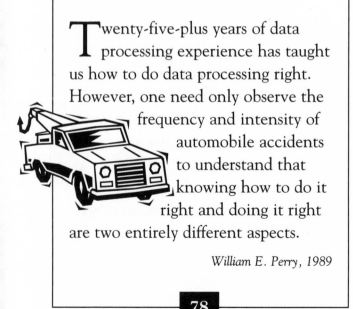

William E. Perry, 1989

Managers who are empire builders often command huge salaries and astronomical department budgets. Systems analysts are encouraged to design larger and larger systems. Programmers soon learn never to write one line of code when one hundred lines will do the same job just as well.

Joseph Weintraub, 1983

Sometimes a firm goes in for automation about like a young man getting married. He knows he can't justify the step on economic grounds but he just can't resist the temptation.

Walter Buckingham, 1961

I stopped relying on spelling checkers after writing a letter informing a supplier that we would look forward to suing their services.

Anonymous

. . . computer executives have always been aware of the human element in programming. Their concern, however, has usually been with eliminating, rather than understanding, the human element.

Gerald M. Weinberg, 1971

When Things Go Wrong

The most useful word in any computer language is "oops." Stuff happens. Bad stuff. Sometimes there's a bit of warning—the hard drive starts making random grinding sounds, or the word processor stps typng crtn lttrs. At other times, the disaster strikes with the suddenness of a sneeze. One moment, you're happily updating the home inventory; the next moment, you're on hold waiting to hear that the problem isn't under warranty.

Yea, from the table of my memory
I'll wipe away all trivial fond
records . . .

Hamlet, experiencing a system crash in 1603

**For most people today,
computers are like an
appendix: nothing to think
about until it gives us
trouble.**

Edward A. Feigenbaum, 1983

Word cannot edit the unknown.

Error message from Word 6.0, 1993

Passwords *are* good at one thing, though. They let you shoot yourself in the foot, real good. They practically load the gun, cock the hammer for you, and beg you to pull the trigger.

Woody Leonhard, 1994

Twain error . . .

WinFax error message, indicating something is off twack, 1992

A fine calculation you are making! It is plain you don't know the ins and outs of the printers . . .

Don Quixote, dealing with an early interfacing problem, as quoted by Miguel de Cervantes, 1615

Too often a simple computer pretending to be a fancy one gets stuck in the "Turing Tar Pit" and is of no use if the results are needed in less than a million years.

Alan Kay, 1984

Printers are not intended to work the first time you set them up. If they do, it is because you didn't follow instructions.

Joel Makower, 1984

Unfortunately, the silliest and the tiniest oversights may cause agonizing hours of delay. "Down time" may apply equally to the machine and to your state of mind.

Dorthea Atwater, 1985

Let the Games Begin

Thirty seconds after the first computer was created, some lab assistant started using it to play a game. The name of the game is lost to history, but most experts believe it was called "Switch me on, switch me off." Moments later, someone made an unauthorized copy, even though there was no second computer available. Since that time, games have become a big business. Unfortunately, business still hasn't become a game.

Never overestimate the intelligence or underestimate the reflexes of the average game player.

Anonymous slogan heard frequently in the halls of early video game companies, circa 1983

. . . there are so many other uses of the microcomputer waiting to be discovered, but most of the potential discoverers are too busy playing games to consider alternative uses.

Robert M. Tripp, 1980

I still think there's no music as sweet as the noise of the Playland arcade at 48th and Broadway with all the games going at once. It's like being in an electronic rain forest.

James Gorman, 1985

The play's the thing.

William Shakespeare, giving what is believed to be the first computer game review, 1603

Once you forget that their main purpose is to play games, you start getting into trouble.

Tom Roginski, 1994

I can always write my own program if I want to, of course. But that's like cutting down a tree and sawing it into blocks and sanding them in order to play with building blocks.

Orson Scott Card, 1983

The danger of computer catatonia increases with the level of sophistication of the computer games. As the complexities unfold in front of the enraptured player, the replies to external influence of, "I'll be there in a minute," become less frequent and more feeble. The addicts to computer games are afflicted with rapture of the beep.

Jack M. Nilles, 1982

88

I don't think it makes sense to distinguish too strictly between teaching programs and games. If a teaching program is good, it feels like a game; if a game is good, it teaches you things.

Arthur Naiman, 1983

If a computer lets you win, it is not because the computer likes you or feels pity for you, but because it has been programmed to let you win.

Marvin Grosswirth, 1978

Computer technology for the next 30 years will be driven by the entertainment industry.

Ed McCracken, CEO of Silicon Graphics, 1994

. . . the first manifestation of the Computer Revolution will be loaded with gimmickry. Man is highly motivated to own and operate toys and gadgets.

Christopher Evans, 1979

We have a great capacity for developing a splendid technology and then wasting it on inane frivolities.

F. J. M. Laver, 1980

Kids

The folk singer Pete Seeger once said that every child should be issued a banjo at birth. Along those lines, every computer should come equipped with a child. After the kid installs your new printer driver and shows you how to undelete the files you accidentally trashed, she'll probably also be happy to set the clock on your VCR. Remember, when the little moppet grins, giggles, and says, "It's really easy," she isn't trying to make you feel old, slow, and stupid. Besides, where else can you hire a consultant for a quarter?

Undeniably, some kids click with computers. The emphasis, however, belongs on *some*—as in the phrase, *some* kids click with violins, or *some* kids click with paintbrushes. But there are no millions being spent to bring violins or paintbrushes into the schools.

Theodore Roszak, 1986

The only possible way that I can justify feeding pages of a book through a computer to a computer terminal is that the younger generation has been hypnotized by television and is willing to read only if the material appears on a screen.

John G. Kemeny, 1972

Children are delighted to think of a computer as a stupid but speedy slave working for a smart but slow master.

Stephen D. Savas, 1985

. . . traditionally, the arrogance of youth was countered by the arrogance of experience. Now, both arrogances are on the same side. It is not your side.

W. Lambert Gardiner, 1987

One of the reasons that children learn to swim in the computer-ized pool so quickly is that here, at least, they have no fear of drowning.

Peter Stoler, 1984

Caution: Only use this program under child supervision.

Alison Lubar, 1994

Take an apple to my teacher? But my teacher *is* an Apple.

John Simon, discussing computers in education, 1986

Even during the short time in which microcomputers have been available, there is already overwhelming evidence that most children are so attracted to computers that they will use them for anything, even for learning.

Elisabeth Gerver, 1986

Forecasts from the Past

Sticking your neck out is a dangerous game, as demonstrated frequently during the French revolution. Some predictions are frighteningly accurate. Others are just frightening. It's a lot safer to let others predict and then pass judgement from the comfort of the present. Shall we?

. . . predicting the future is extraordinarily difficult, whether attempting to do it with the aid of crystal balls, chicken entrails, common sense, or a high-speed digital computer.

Tom Logsdon, 1985

Late in the 1940's, credence was given to the forecast that a dozen high speed computers would be able to handle all the calculations required in the United States.

John Diebold, 1969

I see a world market for about five computers.

Attributed to Thomas J. Watson, Sr., former leader of IBM, circa 1947

Frankly, I couldn't see this gigantic, costly, unreliable device as a piece of business equipment.

Thomas J. Watson, Jr., former CEO of IBM, describing his reaction to ENIAC, 1990

There is no reason for any individual to have a computer in their home.

Ken Olsen, former president of DEC, 1977. At the time he said this, he was probably absolutely right.

There is no technical reason why someone like Sears Roebuck should not come out tomorrow with an appliance selling for less than a TV set, capable of being plugged in wherever there is electricity, and giving immediate access to all information needed for schoolwork from first grade through college.

Peter F. Drucker, anticipating Prodigy by a couple decades, 1968

Computing power will come in much the same way that water, gas, electricity, and telephones are provided today.

Nigel Calder, predicting a new utility, 1969

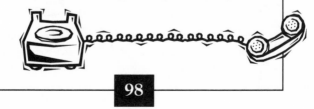

Ironically, neither Huxley nor Orwell predicted the coming of computers. In fact, of all the technologies anticipated by philosophers during the past two centuries, perhaps none has been less predicted than the computer.

Eugene F. Provenzo, 1986

E ven error has its uses.

Alvin Toffler, discussing the need to
make predictions, 1970

Instruction manuals will shrink from ten inches to ten pages. Software will be virtually self-operating. Few users will need to have any understanding of computer hardware or computer languages to operate these machines.

Philip E. Rollhaus, 1986

Waiting in Line to Go On-line

Get ready for the electronic superhypeway. It's just around the corner. Honk if you love clichés, bad puns, or new names for old ideas. The road is splattered with Gore, but everyone is hopping on the bandwagon. Most of the good words have already been taken. Can a product named "lug nuts" be far away? Here's a simple experiment you can do at home. Instead of screaming "The Infobahn is coming!" try shouting "They're building a really big library in town and it won't just have books, it will also have lots of stuff from people who have nothing better to do than to write messages." Still excited?

Can't the Internet's recent runaway growth be explained mostly by its being approximately *free* to millions of new personal computer users?

Bob Metcalfe, 1994

Depending on whom you talk to, the highway could be the biggest leap in human communications since Sputnik, or simply more sour cream and chives for America's couch potatoes.

Daniel Tynan, 1994

Within any community of 20 million people, there's bound to be a red-light district.

Brian Behlendorf, commenting on pornography on the Internet, 1994

A couple of weeks ago, I wrote a story in which I noted that when it comes to cable television, traffic does not appear to be bumper to bumper on the information superhighway. I winced as I wrote that line and was overcome with remorse sometime later because I had just contributed to a wave of metaphor-abuse.

Robert Siegel, 1993

Let Bill Gates pay for it.

*John Edwards, suggesting
a simple way to fund the
information superhighway, 1994*

When you create the mega-metaphor of information superhighway, you are just begging for piling on. So I think when it comes to the information superhighway, we should just pile into the RV and just load up the roof racks with metaphors and have a ball.

Jeff Greenfield, 1993

Cyberspace, in its present condition, has a lot in common with the 19th Century West. It is vast, unmapped, culturally and legally ambiguous, verbally terse (unless you happen to be a court stenographer), hard to get around in, and up for grabs.

John Perry Barlow, 1990

The Information Superhighway is a misnomer. First, there's no highway—there are no roadmaps, guides, rules. And second, it ain't super.

David Martin, 1994

105

Like a new road that can bring fresh life to a remote area or merely make it easier for the local population to leave, the information network is a two-way system.

Nigel Calder, 1969

Naturally, I've resigned myself to being bypassed by the big ethereal interstate like some rundown motel on old neglected Route 66. When two-year-olds are E-mailing their first defiant "No!" to their parents at work, I'll be the last person in America still licking stamps.

Owen Edwards, 1993

I t's a crude but effective cross between a chain letter and a shouting match.

Andrew Kantor, describing Internet mailing lists, 1994

Everything you need to know is on the Internet. You just can't find it.

Anonymous, but common knowledge to anyone who's been there

T he frontier is getting so crowded that no one goes there anymore.

Esther Dyson (paraphrasing Yogi Berra) on cyberspace, 1994

Considered as a piece of cable, the Internet is like a very long string to which millions of tin cans are attached.

Bennett Falk, 1994

Unlike any previous medium, the Net's speed and reach seem to enable reaction to events that have not yet taken place. But this is an illusion. We are not seeing into the future, but more deeply into the present.

Christopher Locke, 1994

Cast of Characters, Part Two: Programmers

A programmer is an engine that runs on pizza and takeout Szechuan, works non-stop for up to several days without rest, and produces millions of lines of code—some of which do what they're supposed to do, but all of which do something. The average programmer owns five calculators, two pairs of jeans, and no combs. The above-average programmer comes equipped pretty much the same way except that he has only one pair of jeans. There are corporate programmers who wear a suit and tie, but they can write only one line of code a day when fettered with such trappings.

Computer programmers are among the great innovators of our times. Unhappily, among their most enduring accomplishments are several new techniques for wasting time.

Robert Jourdain, 1986

All programmers are optimists. Perhaps this modern sorcery especially attracts those who believe in happy endings and fairy godmothers.

Frederick P. Brooks, Jr., 1975

Many programmers think that programming is so wonderful, so elegant, so fun, that anyone who does not want to become a programmer must be a few bricks shy of a load. This is roughly analogous to a happy stable cleaner failing to comprehend why *every*one doesn't enjoy shoveling manure as much as he does.

John Bear, 1983

It's a big boost to the ego to write code that works and that nobody else can read. It's bad practice, but often almost irresistible.

Jim Butterfield, 1983

Software design is an engineering profession—at least that's what we software types like to claim. Actually, it's an aspiration to a profession.

Boris Beizer, 1986

People program for a variety of reasons. One, of course, is that they get paid to do so.

Raymond S. Nickerson, 1986

As soon as you start kludging it, you know you're just about there.

Gene Sewell on software design, 1994

Marginal practitioners are seldom forced out of the software market; instead they move on to another employer (and receive an increase in pay in the process, of course).

Robert Laurence Baber, 1982

Writing a complex program which is free of errors is a task that can drive people insane.

Adrian Berry, 1983

The Big Boys

There are shining corporate giants whose names represent all that is fine and great in our country. Through innovation and excellence in product development, these few companies have become the ideal toward which all competitors strive. Unfortunately, McDonald's and Wendy's don't make computers yet, so it would be quite a stretch to include them in this section. Fortunately, there has always been a lot of talk about IBM, Apple, Microsoft, and the other big players, so this section does not have to be left blank.

Indeed, the IBM personal computer is more Intel's standard and Microsoft's standard than it is IBM's standard.

Regis McKenna, 1989

Obsolete power corrupts obsoletely.

Ted Nelson, on the IBM PC being the industry standard, 1987

Some of my best friends own IBMs.

John J. Anderson, 1984

Eating our own
dogfood . . .

*A phrase used by Bill Gates
and also by Steve Ballmer to
describe the Microsoft
philosophy of using their own
products, 1992*

Since we built such sophisticated
business machines, people tended
to think of IBM as a model of order
and logic—a totally streamlined
organization in which we developed
plans rationally and carried them out
with utter precision. I never thought
for a minute that was really the case.

Thomas J. Watson, Jr., 1990

116

My view of Microsoft is that they had two goals in the last 10 years: to copy the Macintosh and to copy Lotus' success in the applications business. And they accomplished those goals. Now, they're kind of lost.

Steve Jobs, 1994

. . . it is our ultimate goal to eliminate the need for a customer to do his own programming.

Trip Hawkins, founder of Electronic Arts, speaking as Apple Computer's Manager of Business Marketing, 1979

Except for one or two outposts in their early, independent days, IBM was never a sexy company. It hires attractive, energetic young men and women, but expects them to leave each other completely alone.

Nancy Foy, 1975

It was Camelot in Cupertino; Shangri La in Silicon Valley. Apple had the corporate atmosphere of a toy store at Christmas time.

Stephen T. McClellan, 1984

Employees of the Mac project had to endure Job's endless string of get-the-work-done-quickly demands. He seemed a cross between a football coach and Chairman Mao.

Robert Slater, 1987

 The Macintosh enthusiasts grew in numbers by the day while sullen PC owners looked enviously at the wonders denied them.

R. Wayne Parker, 1990

119

Stick 'em Up, I've Got a Modem: Computer Crime

When it comes to crime, "PC" definitely does not stand for "petty cash." Criminal masterminds, some of whom are actually old enough to drive, have deflected several mega-billion dollars from the electronic cash stream. Eventually, some of that money will be missed. By then, it will all have been spent on Twinkies™ and birch beer. While the greedy are using computers to commit electronic carjacking, those motivated by other needs are committing crimes against the computer. Some criminals attack through software, most commonly with a virus. Others use hardware, the most common example being a sledgehammer.

The typical computer con artist tends to be precisely the kind of employee you would want on your payroll if you could keep him from dipping his fingers in the till.

Tom Logsdon, 1985

But the law is slow and the computer fast.

Milton R. Wessel, *commenting on the failure of the law to keep up with technological change, 1974*

Crime usually does its ingenious best to keep pace with technology . . .

Thomas Whiteside, 1978

Computer-literate people do in fact possess an arsenal of nifty gadgets and techniques that would allow them to conceal all kinds of exotic skullduggery, and if they could only *shut up* about it, they could probably get away with all manner of amazing information crimes.

Bruce Sterling, 1992

The modern thief can steal more with a computer than with a gun. Tomorrow's terrorist may be able to do more damage with a keyboard than with a bomb.

From a National Research Council report, December 1990

Computers have created opportunities for crime that never existed before. The rapid spread of personal computer terminals and distributed processing have made high-tech rip-offs much easier for all grades of white-collar worker. The new technology is thus *democratizing* white-collar crime, because it enables even the humblest programmer or operator to participate in illegal activities that were once pretty much the preserve of top management.

Tom Forester, 1987

Today's computer systems are like bodies with skins but no immune systems, or like walled cities without police.

Hans Moravec, discussing viruses, 1988

In prison criminals learn new skills that are highly adaptable to forgery, counterfeiting, lock picking, and safe cracking. Why not teach them programming as well?

Donn B. Parker, 1976

Maybe it says something about human nature that the only form of life we have created so far is purely destructive. Talk about creating life in our own image.

Stephen Hawking, discussing the possibility that computer viruses should be considered life forms, 1994

Artificial Intelligence

Can machines think? Let's ask the computer. It will know. Actually, it doesn't really matter if computers can think. What matters is whether we think they can think. Of course, if they think that we think that they think, then we might think differently about them.

. . . any computer with powers comparable with the brain would have to occupy a fair-sized office building, if not a skyscraper.

Norbert Wiener, the father of cybernetics, 1964

Man does not live by problem solving alone. Artificial intelligence will not only help us with solving problems, but will also give us freedom and leisure for exercising those human qualities which computers cannot touch.

Freeman J. Dyson, a starter on the physicists' all-star team, 1988

Well, you've just got to outthink it.

Marion Tinsley, champion checkers player,
on his strategy in a tournament against
the latest computer challenger, 1994

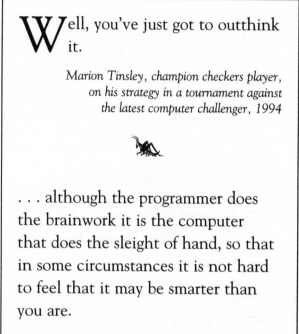

. . . although the programmer does the brainwork it is the computer that does the sleight of hand, so that in some circumstances it is not hard to feel that it may be smarter than you are.

Scott Corbett, 1980

I hate it when computer programs think they're smarter than I am.

Woody Leonhard, 1994

With the advent of the microprocessor chip has come the unbridled application of the adjective "smart" to anything that contains one.

John J. Simon, 1986

Yet to calculate is not in itself to analyze.

Edgar Allan Poe, 1841

They have love but they also have typewriters.

Racter, a conversational computer program created by William Chamberlain and Thomas Etter, circa 1984

128

Even if it's possible to write a computer program that simulates paranoid behavior well enough to fool many psychiatrists, that may still be a superficial way to learn about paranoia.

Katharine Davis Fishman, 1981

Clearly, we require a machine that has enough "brains" to stay clear of cliffsides. But, on the other hand, we don't want one that "thinks" too independently or it will never agree to make the trip in the first place.

Alfred J. Cote, Jr., discussing the problem of designing an intelligent robot to explore Mars, 1967

What if computers tell us something we do not like or do not want to know about the universe? If we create super-intelligent computers to probe the mysteries of the universe, then we should be prepared for the possibility that what they have to tell us may be intellectually shocking or emotionally unacceptable.

Christopher Evans, 1979

Superintelligence is not perfection—spectacular failures are certain.

Hans Moravec, 1988

Even if computers are writing prize-winning novels and discovering new mathematical theorems, we'll still argue over who should get the credit, us or them.

George Johnson, 1986

Big Brother Has a Lot of Hardware: Computers and the Government

Uncle Sam no longer wants you—he already has you. Fortunately, he isn't sure where he put you. Think of the government's computers as a giant roach trap—data gets in but it can't get out. Besides, Big Brother is probably too busy looking for ways to replace the trillion dollars the government spent on computers that became obsolete before the red ink dried on the contracts.

Computerization has not made the federal government more efficient; rather, it has merely magnified the impact of its snafus.

August Bequai, 1987

There is no such thing as electronic privacy.

Winn Schwartau, 1994

. . . the computer is forcing us to reformulate the very distinction between public and private acts.

Abbe Mowshowitz, 1976

Even the NSA and CIA can't break into Compuserve's computers. I understand it's because the computers are so old that nobody can remember how to.

Tim Wilson, reassuring a correspondent concerning the security of e-mail, 1994

It's a "phase change"—like moving from ice to water. Ice is simple and water is simple, but in the middle of the change it's mush—part monopoly, part franchise, part open competition. We want to manage that transition.

Al Gore on the role of government in the development of a National Information Interchange, 1993

To protect itself from the litigious envy of less successful organizations, such as the U.S. government, IBM employs 68 percent of all known ex-attorneys general.

Stan Kelly-Bootle, 1981

. . . today, I learned to turn one on . . .

George Bush, updating the press on his quest for computer literacy in the highest reaches of government, 1991

What's a mouse?

Presidential spokesman Marlin Fitzwater, in response to the question of whether the president's computer had a mouse, 1991

Jargon and Hype

While others have delved into alphanumeric amalgamation, our hardcopy morph of the ASCII paradigm is state-of-the-art. Using Eye-Directed Interstitial-Text Optical-Recognition Software™, an errorless throughput with high tactile enjoyment has been constructed for retro-fit into any vertically-oriented, freestanding, spatial storage device. We are also pleased to point out that the following quotes are easily the most spectacular ever collected. A huge research and development effort, heavily funded by some of the top venture capitalists in Silicon Valley, has resulted in a unique product. Our *NEW SOLAR MODEL* requires NO EXTERNAL ELECTRICITY OR BATTERIES!!! Supplies are limited.

I don't understand a word you're saying, but it sounds great.

Television executive Mr. Azae to
computer designer Richard Sumner in
the movie "Desk Set," 1957

You may have read that the uses for some piece of hardware or software are "limited only by your imagination." View any such claim with a severely jaundiced eye, not only because it raises the suspicion that the writer couldn't think of any good uses in time for the deadline, but also because it simply isn't true.

Van Wolverton, 1986

Computer publications are filled with articles, mostly written by academic theoreticians, on the latest esoteric concepts in computer architecture. The authors, who have never been responsible for building anything that *works*, are convincing.

David E. Lundstrom, 1988

The necromancy of the Internet is tempting; the possibilities it yields enchanting. But when the clock strikes midnight, the prince will become a frog. The smoke and mirrors will go away. My electronic message to you: Don't believe the hype.

Ben Rothke, 1994

Everyone from a well-meaning but starry-eyed press to the refrigerator salesmen who found themselves selling disk drives  instead of ice-cube makers firmly believed that personal computers could do almost anything in the hands of almost anyone.

Arlan R. Levitan, 1984

The computer is the most beautiful and useful of man's inventions. The manufacturers' brochures say so.

Robert M. Baer, 1972

There is so much unexplored territory that manufacturers are going off in hundreds of different directions, each claiming to be the best, fastest, most reliable, and most economical of all. Whatever is true about what they say today is almost certain not to be true next week.

Richard M. Koff, 1979

Multimedia is a buzzword.

Philippe Kahn, founder of Borland International, 1993

But until you come into contact with computer software, you have no true appreciation of the glorious heights to which jargon can rise or how great a barrier it can become to normal human communications.

Harry Kleinberg, 1977

. . . let's resolve to take a break from the entire concept of virtual anything unless we want folks to think we're nothing more than consultants attempting to generate a living by making other people feel more stupid than we actually are.

Gil Schwartz, 1994

Newsletters are a goldmine of technobabble—and subscribing to one may require a goldmine.

John A. Barry, 1992

There is no significant issue pertaining to computer technology that cannot be described clearly in plain English and understood by real estate brokers, sculptors and teachers of nineteenth-century French literature; moreover, democracy assumes that janitors and taxi drivers can comprehend important political questions, and computer technology does not present any compelling reason to abandon that assumption.

Katharine Davis Fishman, 1981

142

It Must Be True— The Computer Said So

In the early seventies, you could have your handwriting analyzed by a computer on the boardwalk at Seaside Heights, New Jersey. That's what the sign promised. Actually, the machine was not a computer, but just a card sorter. And the analysis was pure bunk. But we are extremely willing to accept higher truths from anywhere, and especially from things we don't fully understand. Granted, the computer is slightly more reliable than the Magic Eightball when given the proper data, but so is the average nine-year-old. Even a coin toss is right half the time.

143

The self-fulfilling prophesy is one of the great psychological truths of human life. Nothing about computers prevents them from verifying that the world is the way you want to believe it is.

Michael Crichton, 1983

Of all the traps PCs can lead us into, none is so pernicious as the tendency to automatically accept as gospel anything that comes out of a computer.

Jim Seymour, 1991

There are four canonical forms of the lie: commission, omission, statistics, graphs. And now there is also Visicalc.

Jean-Louis Gassée, 1987

The worst thing that ever happened to entrepreneurs was the invention of Lotus 1-2-3. They no longer have to think about the business. All they do is come up with three or four alternative ways in general that things could happen. Then they plug in the numbers and have a blinding flash of data.

Don Valentine, 1993

People must understand they are the ultimate backup to the computer. And they have the responsibility to make sure their decision is correct, regardless of what the computer is telling them.

Leonard Lee, 1992

We offer them mediocrity while calling it magic. We offer them the illusion of intelligent software, seducing them into surrendering the task of thinking to the machine. Of course, the machine isn't thinking, which means that nobody is.

Larry Constantine, 1994

I heard a telling comment recently:
If you torture numbers long
enough, you can make them say
anything.

Cheryl Currid, 1994

Forty-two.

*Deep Thought, giving the Answer to the
Great Question of Life, the Universe
and Everything in Douglas Adams's*
The Hitchhiker's Guide to the Galaxy, *1979*

They're Just Like People, Only Different

It's not really a lifeless hunk of electronics. No, it's my buddy, my pal. It's almost human. Honest. We spend lots of time together, getting to know each other. It likes me. It really does. I have to go now; it's waiting for me.

. . . all we have to go on is a suspicion that computers speak a different language from us because they were born somewhere else, like the French.

Phil Bertoni, 1983

Computers are gifted with such a facade of impersonal precision; they have no way to look or sound or act crazy.

Theodore Roszak, 1986

This is man's first encounter outside himself with something that is exactly like some inside part of himself.

Elting E. Morison, 1966

They are not like intelligent horses or dogs, who might someday threaten us; they are more like intelligent corals or sponges, happily content to live in the sea.

T. A. Heppenheimer, 1983

The objective here is a machine that hears so well that it will someday cry out, "Quiet in there, I can't concentrate on these computations!"

Alfred J. Cote, Jr., on the topic of speech recognition, 1967

The reasoning animal has finally made the reasoning machine.

Edward A. Feigenbaum, 1983

If you're reading mail or typing words into a file, your computer is doing next to nothing, not even working up a sweat, stifling yawns. If you are staring at the screen and thinking, or talking on the phone, or doodling, napping, flirting or having lunch—and these are all activities in which (yes) people *continue* to indulge, in flagrant disregard of the powerful computers sitting on their desks—believe it or not—well, under these circumstances, your computer is fighting back tears of boredom.

David Hillel Gelernter, 1991

Carbon life took more than a billion years to progress from single-celled to multicelled creatures. Silicon devices managed something similar in twenty-five years.

O. B. Hardison, Jr., 1989

. . . in poems, in novels, in paintings, the brain seems to find itself able to work well with material that any computer would have to reject as formless.

Norbert Wiener, 1964

You half expect the words "Have a nice datum" to appear.

John A. Barry, commenting on the
Macintosh smiley-face icon, 1992

These computers are so human in their reactions that chess players sitting down to play with one, after a half dozen moves, have begun referring to it no longer as "it" but "he."

Dana L. Thomas, 1967

. . . you don't know in advance the consequences of what you tell a computer to do; therefore its behavior can be as baffling and surprising and unpredictable to you as that of a person.

Douglas R. Hofstadter, 1979

153

The irony is that the brain is outperforming computers with neurons that operate about a million times slower than silicon. And the secret, of course, is in the wiring . . .

M. Mitchell Waldrop, 1987

Local Networks, E-Mail, and the Joys of Being Part of a Bundle

In offices across the land, all those wonderful little personal computers are being hooked together into local networks. This is sort of like having a window in your bathroom. The light is nice and the scenery can be entertaining, but you'll probably spend most of your time making sure the curtains are fully closed. The miracle of instant communication does have its down side. In the past, the company jerk with the bad sense of humor and the compulsion to comment on everything was easily avoidable. Now, electronic mail is making him an author you can't refuse.

Some software vendors think that even e-mail should be active, doing things unbidden on the recipient's computer, such as launching an application or deleting itself if it lies unread. Sounds like a virus to me.

Larry Constantine, 1994

The Electronic Mail Association estimates that the volume of E-mail will grow by more than half this year, to 6 billion messages. And with my luck, they'll all have my name on them.

Mike Hogan, 1992

156

I haven't had enough E-mail recently and actually had to get some real work done.

Stewart Alsop, after a system problem prevented most of his mail from reaching him, 1994

You want to talk to me, you pick up the phone, you write me, you come into my office. Don't send me E-mail!

Charles Wang, CEO of Computer Associates, 1994

. . . we may be saving trees—but we're starting to drown people.

Esther Dyson on e-mail, 1990

Some network users are simply leery of their system. They're convinced that every document posted to the network might as well be on the Kmart bulletin board.

W. D. Riley, 1994

Unlike print, electronic text defies proverbial wisdom. You can have your cake, give it away, then eat it, and still have it.

Richard A. Lanham, 1993

Having heard stories of E-mail messages vitriolic enough to acid-etch the recipient's monitor, I've decided that people who fume through their word processors feel invulnerable, like little kids shouting challenges and insults to an empty room. Thus, someone can launch a cluster bomb toward a colleague's computer and still be astonished to find that its arrival on target has left the recipient wounded and hungry for revenge.

Owen Edwards, 1993

The Age of Information

Suddenly, we can find out anything almost instantly. The ability has created its own demand. People are seized by a compulsion to know the gross national product of Sudan or the number of hairs in Freud's beard. You can find anything. You can certainly find that there are a lot of people out there who don't like stupid questions. Sadly, there are even more people out there with stupid answers.

It is a sign of the times that many people cannot tell the difference between information and knowledge, not to mention wisdom, which even knowledge tends sometimes to drive out.

Heinz R. Pagels, 1988

I can see some ancient Egyptian philosopher worrying that mankind was entering "The Age of Stretched Rope," an age in which architects would no longer be guided by their good senses and artistic intuition, but by dictates of lengths of stretched rope, counted off impersonally from point to point.

Isaac Asimov, 1968

Maybe I'm unique, but I just don't need more information. I'm drowning in information.

Richard Santalesa, 1993

. . . if you have any money besides what is crumpled in your pocket, it is probably in Cyberspace.

John Perry Barlow, 1991

Computer printers, COMs, CRTs, and other output devices can release more information, most of it trivial, than *all* your employees placed end to end and reading continually can handle.

A. N. Feldzamen, 1971

The impact of cheap, reliable, fast, and universally available information will easily be as great as was the impact of electricity.

Peter F. Drucker, 1968

The world is moving from the Industrial Age into the Information Age so fast we've almost stopped noticing it.

Diane LeBold, 1983

Time and again, in my experience, when I ask for data . . . the answer is, "The data are in the computer." And there they sit.

W. Edwards Deming, 1990

The Industry

At the current rate of growth, there will soon be one computer for each person on the planet (not counting palmtops, personal information managers, and old TRS 80's). We will all have jobs and we will all buy each other's products. The only essential people left outside the industry will be BMW dealers, bartenders, and divorce lawyers.

Because the computer is a universal machine, it creates specialists faster than any previous discovery.

Ben Ross Schneider, 1974

If an industry is booming, can litigation be far behind?

Joel Dreyfuss, commenting on lawsuits against keyboard manufacturers, 1994

The trouble with rabbits is they tend to overdo a good thing. So, too, with microcomputer manufacturers.

Jacqueline Thompson, 1985

165

Shareware is a wonderful little economy, but the honor system works only for things that are cheap, and it's hard to get really rich on things that are cheap.

Peter Huber, 1993

Looking at the personal computer market has been likened to observing the game of rugby for the first time. There's lots of pushing and shoving in evidence, but it's difficult to make out exactly what's going on.

Tom Forester, 1987

Robots can make an auto factory marvelously productive— but they don't buy cars.

M. Mitchell Waldrop, 1987

The media are not toys; they should not be in the hands of Mother Goose and Peter Pan executives.

Marshall McLuhan, 1969

While the PC industry likes to take credit for having invented everything, it has not invented so much as it has borrowed.

Dennis Allen, 1994

For the computer industry, the *l*-word (*layoff*) is the crazy aunt down in the basement—there's no way to get rid of  her, and you know she's going to pop her head up sooner or later.

Steve Evangelou, 1994

One always fears that in certain corporate environments Thomas Edison might not have had the freedom to invent the light bulb. Instead, Mr. Edison might have come up with—a bigger candle.

Philip E. Rollhaus, 1986

The highly competitive ethos in the computer industry sits oddly beside the claim that the use of computers encourages collaborative and cooperative patterns of work.

Elisabeth Gerver, 1986

You've got to feel sorry for the small group within the computer industry that actually has to face the end user.

Eri Golembo, 1990

Intruder Alert— The Computer in Human Affairs

Computers, directly or indirectly, may be responsible for the breakup of more relationships than *Playboy* magazine, the NFL, and *The Feminine Mystique* combined. Some people end up loving their computer more than any form of carbon-based life. People who once had a perfectly normal existence can suddenly spend all their quality time running projections to see what would happen if they switched to a less expensive brand of mustard and only showered every other day. Let's move out of the room, where it can't overhear us, and whisper, "It's only a machine."

Well, are you still divorced from the same wife, or is it a new one?

Standard Silicon Valley greeting at the bar in Rickey's Hotel, as reported by Hans J. Queisser, 1988

People are more important than computers.

Michael Crichton, 1983

The recent birth of the new civilization in Silicon Valley heralds an end to romantic love as it has been known in Western civilization.

Craig Brod, 1984

171

Pierre felt himself to be an insignificant chip fallen among the wheels of a machine  whose action he did not understand but which was working well.

Leo Tolstoy, one of the few authors whose books are as big as computer magazines, in War and Peace, *1869*

One of the things you can learn from history is that men have lived with machinery at least as well as, and probably a good deal better than, they have yet learned to live with one another.

Elting E. Morison, 1966

172

When machines are in league with men, the soul of the alliance must be human, lest its ends become less than human.

John Diebold, 1969

Technology marches on, over you or through you, take your pick.

Stewart Brand, 1987

It certainly seemed foolish to watch a dozen or more people trying to be sexy via keyboard, when separated by thousands of miles of wire.

Clark L. Stewart, describing his first impression of an on-line CB network, 1982

One has to remember, when considering the potential dehumanizing effect of computers, that being human isn't always such a noble thing.

James Gorman, 1985

Say "Buy Buy"

Buying a computer is almost like having a baby. It's an expensive and emotional experience, and once you get it home you don't have a clue what to do with it. Then the fun really starts. Is the $800 modem really that much better than the $50 item? (Odds are that neither will work, so experts advise going with the cheaper model.) Is it better to buy a laser printer or get a less-expensive ink jet printer and invest the savings in soybean futures? Welcome to the consuming passion.

Like it or not, the Computer Age is upon us, and it's here for good. You might as well get used to it, because it's going to cost you money, now, tomorrow, and probably for many years to come.

R. Wayne Parker, 1990

I've shared the common, almost typical, experience of waiting with money in my pocket while a "sales representative" ignored me in favor of hunching over a keyboard to blast bogies in *F-15 Strike Eagle*.

Mark Alvarez, 1990

Do not worry about your future computer becoming obsolete. It will happen no matter what you buy or how long you wait to buy one.

Lincoln Hallen, 1984

Like cameras, sailboats, and bicycles, computers tend to become considerably more expensive over time than their sticker prices would seem to suggest.

Steven K. Roberts, 1984

Once you've decided you need or want a personal computer, prepare to weep.

Barry Owen, 1991

No, I think the cheapest computer we carry costs about $900.

Salesperson at an electronics store, when asked if he had any 486 computers in stock, 1994

All of our representatives are currently assisting a customer.

Order-line voice message for a computer supply company, 1994. Whoever that customer is, he must feel very special.

Assembling microcomputers consists mainly of repetitive tasks such as soldering connections. The project is the electronic equivalent of painting by numbers.

Howard Hillman, on building your own computer from a kit, 1985

. . . when the manufacturer of computers claims flexibility for his machines, he is underlining an indisputable truth. With equal plausibility the truck manufacturer may claim flexibility for his trucks because they can carry canned beef, books, electrolytic condensers, or pumpkins.

Roberto Vacca, 1973

Don't buy a $10,000 solid gold sledge-hammer to drive in a two-cent thumb tack.

John Bear, 1983

The machine puzzles us less than the demand for it.

Richard A. Lanham, 1993

Buying a computer is very much like buying a car. That is, first you have to establish in your own mind that you *need* a car!

Byron G. Wels, 1978

What Is a Computer?

W hat exactly is a computer? It's a thinking machine that doesn't really think. It's an expensive hunk of business equipment that plays great games. It's a piece of home electronics that few homes need but most homes want. The computer has so many aspects that it is hard to define. Maybe it's a mirror. Maybe it's a walrus. Let's sample the possibilities . . .

Some computers are like cats or court judges—you can tell them things, but you can't tell them much, even using what you believe to be the correct language.

Lincoln Hallen, 1984

. . . a computer (mildly) resembles a painter who insists on attacking the Empire State Building with a makeup-daubing brush. But if you are a computer this strategy is sound, and you will complete the job much faster than an army of humans equipped with industrial-size paint blasters. *Yes*, you are only capable of daubing. But you daub *fast*.

David Hillel Gelernter, 1991

The computer is an extension, a reflection of what we think is important, what oppresses us. Thus an office worker compelled to sit, earplugged and screenbound, without the pleasures of human involvement that make otherwise tedious work bearable, sees the computer very differently from a hacker who can't wait to sit down at the screen.

Pamela McCorduck, 1985

The first digital computer, of course, was a set of ten fingers that somebody realized could be used for counting.

Gene DeWeese, 1984

For the computer is a big brain in its most elementary state: a gigantic octopus, fed with symbols instead of crabs.

Lewis Mumford, 1966

Computers enable us to communicate with ourselves (a curious achievement) as well as with friends, colleagues, machines, and completely anonymous others.

Michael R. Real, 1989

Computers are a lot like the Old Testament view of God—lots of rules and not very forgiving.

Joseph Campbell, 1987

If you don't mind waiting billions of years for your answer, and if you have plenty of extra disks or tapes for memory, any digital computer is as good as any other.

Rudy Rucker, 1987

Did we invent the computer because we needed very fast calculators, or did the calculators suggest to us the importance of solving problems that require such speed?

J. David Bolter, 1984

Using One

When you buy a car, you just have to drive it. When you buy a television, you just have to watch it. But when you buy a computer, you have to use it. The more you use it, the less expensive it becomes. This is known as amortizing the cost. Until the computer came along, this technique was mostly used with home exercise equipment, pianos, and bass boats. It doesn't really work, but it makes you feel better. Using a computer can be a lot of fun as long as you remember two simple rules. 1. Don't use it for anything important because you can't really trust it. 2. Don't waste the awesome power of the machine on trivial applications.

186

PCs are the world's greatest medium for futzing around. They're computational catnip for obsessives, keyboard crack for neurotics and seductive time sinks for ordinary folk who just want to make sure that they've reasonably examined all their options. Why do you think we call them "users"?

Michael Schrage, 1994

It doesn't matter how acquainted you are with a particular brand of computer. When you need to borrow someone else's, it feels like you're using their toothbrush.

Kevin Kelly, 1994

Why does it take a computer magazine 6–8 weeks to change your address when you move? Don't they use computers?

John McCormick, 1990

You mean I can put a different disk in the computer? You're kidding.

A user who had kept the same floppy in her computer for over a year, 1993

On mechanical slavery, on the slavery of the machine, the future of the world depends.

Oscar Wilde, 1895

Some people learn to use computers in ritual ways. Without necessarily understanding what they are doing, they go through a sequence of steps to make a computer "magically" respond. Computer technology appears to them as one of the mysterious forces of the universe.

Judith A. Perrolle, 1987

I don't know anything about computers, and when I am around them all they say is stupid things like 01001100100101101.

George Goodman, writing as "Adam Smith," 1967

If you are like most people, your relationship with computers is stuck in early adolescence. It's like the seventh-grade dance in your school gym. The girls were on one side, the boys on the other. Now you're on one side, and computers are on the other.

Fred D'Ignazio, 1984

You can't fail to get along with a computer; it will never turn on you, it will never insist on talking about what it wants to talk about or doing what it wants to do. It will never find you boring, never forget to call, never ask a favor.

Gregg Easterbrook, 1983

> *The moment I win the lottery, my computer becomes the world's most expensive boat anchor.*
>
> Jacques Hughes, 1992

Nothing, it often seems to us, can be done *without* the computer. Nothing, it frequently seems, can be done *with* the computer.

Jack M. Nilles, 1982

Once you have written a program that makes the computer perform satisfactorily, you *know* who's boss.

Scott Corbett, 1980

About half the tutorial manuals I've read don't tell you how to stop. That's like teaching a driver without telling him where the brakes are.

Boris Beizer, 1986

There are no built-in checks in a computer to see where you got your education, if you have one, or whether your socks match.

Joseph Deken, 1981

Cast of Characters, Part Three: Hackers and Nerds

"Hacker" is a good word gone bad. It used to mean someone who lived to push a computer to its limits. Now it means someone who breaks into computer systems. A nerd is someone who knows how to do this, but doesn't have the nerve to try. Both groups will be annoyed at being placed together, even if only on paper.

Most hackers have a greater interest in Calvin Klein than Karl Marx.

August Bequai, 1987

. . . I could fake enough computing to impress astronomers, and maybe pick it up fast enough that my co-workers wouldn't catch on. Still, a computer wizard? Not me—I'm an astronomer.

Clifford Stoll, who broke a German spy ring that had infiltrated American computer networks, 1989

Fear of hackers in a virtual community is a little like fear of pyromaniacs in a rice-paper city.

Howard Rheingold, 1993

With computers getting more popular and complex, industry experts predict a growing need for computer nerds. In fact, one industry group forecasts a nerd gap in the coming years as demand outstrips supply.

Jamie McIntyre, *reporting on Rent-A-Nerd, 1992*

Version numbers are a relic from the PC's nerdy past, when engineers designed and developed software for people who secretly wanted to be engineers.

Ed Bott, 1994

They were a pale, sickly-looking crowd by L.A. standards, but unlike the surfers and the Hollywood dreamers, they asked smart questions in class and had something to talk about besides themselves. I figured they knew something I didn't.

Sandra L. Kurtzig, describing the nerds she met at UCLA, 1991

Cops are skilled at getting people to talk, and computer people, given a chair and some sustained  attention, will talk about their computers till their throats go raw.

Bruce Sterling, on techniques for tracking down hackers, 1992

M ost technical people are
genetically incapable of
teaching simple tasks.

W. D. Riley, 1994

README.TXT
or A Few
More Bugs

We thought we had all the bug quotes together. We were sure of it. Positive. But a few seemed to have slipped past, despite hours and hours of testing. Rather than force the user to order an update so soon after publication, we decided to stick them here where no one would notice.

Aprogram can work properly a thousand times and fail suddenly the next time. It might thereby give the appearance of having worn out, but what really happened is that an unusual set of circumstances was encountered for the first time. A program doesn't fail because you wear it out; it fails because it didn't work properly to begin with and you finally have occasion to notice that fact.

John E. Shore, 1985

It (had) been tested extensively to make sure the software would not have any bugs in it. Frankly, it was a surprise to us.

Joseph Hardiman, president of the National Association of Securities Dealers Inc., when new software failed, shutting down NASD trading for several hours, 1994

199

If the companies and products of the future become more like software of today, what does that promise? Televisions that crash? Cars that freeze up suddenly? Toasters that bomb?

Kevin Kelly, 1994

In the past we would blame Mr. So-and-So at the bank for bank statement errors; then we shifted the blame to the bank; now we just blame the computer at the bank. Mr. So-and-So is delighted at this state of affairs, because even though he is responsible for the computer, he can now also blame the computer; and he often gets away with it.

Donn B. Parker, 1976

There are no small errors in data processing. It is the only field where the omission of a single hyphen can cost a company $18 million.

Joseph Weintraub, 1983

Bugs are generated from the moisture of living animals, as it dries up outside their bodies.

Aristotle, 350 BC

It's not your calculating I think ill of; it's your calculating wrong.

Henry James, *pointing out a glitch in the system*, 1881

201

For every computer error, there are at least two human errors, one of which is blaming it on the computer.

Joel Makower, 1984

Dogs get mange. Horses get the staggers. Soldiers of fortune get malaria and computer programs get errors. Without doubt, error is a disease endemic to software—and a congenital one at that. The infection sets in before the first page of code is written. No computer system has ever been born without it; it's the automaton's answer to Original Sin.

Phil Bertoni, 1983